ZANZIBA

TRAVEL GUIDE

2023

"Exploring the Enchanting Isles: A Comprehensive Zanzibar Travel Guide"

HENRY WAYNE

TABLE OF CONTENT

INTRODUCTION

Welcome to the picturesque archipelago of Zanzibar, a tropical paradise situated off the eastern coast of Africa in the Indian Ocean. With its intriguing combination of history, culture, and natural beauty, Zanzibar has become a sought-after destination for tourists seeking a unique and unforgettable experience.

Zanzibar is consists of two main islands, Unguja and Pemba, together with many smaller islets. Its strategic location along old trade routes has enhanced its legacy, giving it a melting pot of many civilizations, including African, Arab, Indian, and European influences. This cultural blend is visible in its architecture, cuisine, music, and traditional festivals.

The islands have a rich history, with traces of human occupancy reaching back to the 6th century. Throughout the years, Zanzibar has been a hub of trade, attracting traders from throughout the world. In the 19th century, it became a significant hub for the slave trade, having a lasting imprint on its past and present.

Today, Zanzibar offers visitors a wide choice of attractions. The gorgeous beaches with fluffy white sands and crystal-clear seas are great for leisure and water sports lovers alike. Snorkeling and diving show an underwater wonderland of brilliant coral reefs and rich marine life.

Venture into the medieval Stone Town, a UNESCO World Heritage site, and meander through tiny passageways lined with elaborately carved doors and antique structures. Immerse yourself in the bustling local marketplaces, where spices, fabrics, and handicrafts make a sensory feast for the curious tourist.

For nature aficionados, the Jozani Forest is a must-visit, home to the rare red colobus monkeys and an assortment of local flora and wildlife. Discover the island's spice farms and learn about the essential role spices had in molding the island's history and economics.

Zanzibar's kind and hospitable people are as much a feature as its gorgeous landscapes. The people, known as Zanzibaris, will greet you with a grin and embrace you with their hospitality, allowing you to experience the genuine essence of their culture and way of life.

Whether you want relaxation on its exquisite beaches, discovery of its historical riches, or an absorption in its lively culture, Zanzibar guarantees a genuinely unique vacation. So, pack your bags and get ready to be enchanted by the magic of this tropical treasure that continues to cast a spell on everyone who visit.

CHAPTER 1: THE ENCHANTING ARCHIPELAGO

Welcome to the Enchanting Archipelago, a mesmerizing collection of islands where nature weaves a tapestry of wonder and culture dances to the rhythm of centuries-old traditions. This wonderful place, sprinkled like pearls in the turquoise waves of the ocean, welcomes daring spirits and lovers of tranquillity alike.

Each island in this fascinating archipelago provides a unique appeal, yet all share a similar thread of awe-inspiring beauty. Sun-kissed beaches with powdery sands caress the shorelines, urging you to bathe in their warmth and immerse yourself in the turquoise embrace of the sea. Beneath the waters lay hidden riches of vivid coral reefs and a symphony of aquatic life, making it a delight for snorkelers and divers.

Step ashore, and you'll find yourself in a world rich in history and cultural variety. Ancient ruins whisper tales of civilizations past, while towering temples and exquisite architecture serve as testaments to the artistic talent of the local people. The blending of traditions from diverse corners of the globe generates a tapestry of festivals, customs, and rituals that honor the rich legacy of the archipelago.

As you meander through crowded marketplaces, your senses will be tantalized by the perfume of exotic spices, the vivid colors of handcrafted items, and the sounds of active talk in many languages. Indulge in the scrumptious cuisine, where the tastes of fresh seafood, tropical fruits, and fragrant spices mingle together to produce a gourmet experience like no other.

For those who desire to connect with nature, the Enchanting Archipelago offers different landscapes that vary from lush jungles rich with species to mist-covered mountains reaching for the heavens. Hiking routes entice daring individuals to explore the hidden jewels of each island, rewarding them with beautiful panoramas and a profound sense of calm.

But despite its natural beauty and cultural treasures, what truly enchants visitors is the warm welcome and genuine smiles of the residents. Their real openness and enthusiasm to share their way of life make every tourist feel like a beloved guest, leaving an unforgettable impact on their hearts.

Whether you want a peaceful vacation on quiet coastlines, a trip through history and culture, or an expedition into the heart of nature's treasures, the Enchanting Archipelago guarantees an experience that will live in your mind forever. Prepare to be mesmerized as you go on a voyage that will stimulate your senses, nourish your spirit, and leave you wishing to return to the magical embrace of these magnificent islands.

Historical Significance

The historical significance of the Enchanting Archipelago stems in its role as a crossroads of cultures and trade over the millennia. Its strategic location in the Indian Ocean has made it a melting pot of cultures, traditions, and ideas.

One of the most important historical elements is its involvement with the old marine trade routes. The archipelago was a major stop in the spice trade route, which connected the Far East with Africa and Europe. Spices, particularly cloves, were highly sought commodities that attracted traders from all parts of the world, including Arab, Indian, Chinese, and European merchants.

Zanzibar, in particular, acquired importance as a center of the slave trade throughout the 19th century. It became a conduit for the export of slaves from East Africa to numerous destinations, extending a sad chapter in its history. The legacy of the slave trade is still obvious in the historic places and museums that remember this sad history.

The archipelago's history also contains a combination of cultural influences from the Arab, Indian, and European traders and immigrants. This cultural blend is evident in the architecture, language, religion, and food of the islands. The Swahili language, a combination of Bantu and Arabic, arose as a lingua franca in the region and became a vital element of the local identity.

Moreover, the islands were essential in the fight for independence and self-determination. The inhabitants of the archipelago struggled against colonial forces and harsh regimes, seeking autonomy and political independence. These movements had a vital influence in establishing the current character of the islands.

Today, the historical significance of the Enchanting Archipelago is recognized through its UNESCO World Heritage monuments, museums, and cultural events. The preservation of its rich legacy allows tourists to investigate the roots of this compelling location and grasp its role in the greater fabric of human history.

As guests step foot on the islands, they are not merely confronted with natural beauty and great hospitality but also enveloped in the echoes of the past, a reminder of the different civilizations that have left their imprint on the Enchanting Archipelago. By recognising and embracing its historical significance, we may obtain a greater knowledge of the world's interconnectivity and the persistence of the human spirit over the ages.

Cultural Diversity

Zanzibar's cultural richness is an amazing tapestry woven from centuries of interactions between diverse peoples, making it a dynamic and distinctive destination. The archipelago's history as a crossroads of trade routes and a melting pot of civilizations has given rise to a rich and diversified cultural environment.

One of the primary components contributing to Zanzibar's cultural variety is its population, which encompasses diverse ethnic groups. The indigenous population comprises the Bantu-speaking people, like as the Swahili, who have inhabited the islands for generations. Additionally, there are major Arab and Persian influences due to past trade relations, and a sizeable South Asian minority, mostly from India and Pakistan, who migrated in subsequent years.

The Swahili culture is strongly engrained in Zanzibar's identity. It is a unique combination of Bantu and Arab cultures, expressed in the language, food, and traditional rituals. Swahili, as the lingua franca, links individuals from all ethnic origins together, generating a strong sense of togetherness and belonging.

Zanzibar's architecture is a visual monument to its cultural diversity. The tiny, twisting lanes of Stone Town demonstrate a combination of Arabian, Indian, and European architectural traditions. Elaborate wooden doors with complex carvings and beautiful balconies decorate buildings, illustrating the various influences that have molded the island's urban landscape.

Religion has a crucial influence in the cultural fabric of Zanzibar. Islam is the major religion, imported by Arab traders and immigrants several years ago. Mosques and Islamic schools, known as madrassas, may be found across the islands, and the call to prayer vibrates in the air, creating a calm ambiance.

Cultural festivals and festivities give an insight into the heart of Zanzibar's traditions. Events like the Mwaka Kogwa Festival, Eid al-Fitr, and Diwali are celebrated with zeal, bringing communities together to respect their religious beliefs and cultural heritage.

Music and dance are fundamental to Zanzibar's cultural expression. The islands are known for taarab music, a melodic mix of Swahili, Arab, and Indian musical influences. Dances like the ngoma and chakacha are performed on special occasions, offering a look into the region's rich artistic legacy.

Culinary delicacies demonstrate the many influences on Zanzibar's cuisine. Dishes are seasoned with a combination of spices, including cloves, cinnamon, cardamom, and chile, reflecting the island's historical ties to the spice trade. Traditional Zanzibari meals generally blend indigenous ingredients with Arabian and Indian spices, producing a delicious combination of sensations.

In essence, Zanzibar's cultural variety is a stunning symphony of traditions, languages, cuisines, and rituals that have delicately mixed throughout the years. It is a celebration of human connection and a reminder of the beauty that develops when individuals from diverse origins come together to establish a shared identity and a genuinely fascinating location.

CHAPTER 2: PLANNING YOUR TRIP

Best Time to Visit

The ideal time to visit Zanzibar primarily depends on your tastes and what you want to experience during your vacation. Zanzibar boasts a tropical environment, with pleasant temperatures throughout the year, but there are distinct seasons that might impact your trip plans.

Dry Season (June to October): This is considered the finest season to visit Zanzibar. The weather is often drier and colder throughout these months, with lower humidity levels. The sky are bright, and rainfall is light, making it a perfect time for beach activities, water sports, and seeing the historical sites.

Shoulder Season (November to December): November is the beginning of the brief rainy season. While there may be some rainfall, it typically doesn't linger all day. The temperatures stay warm, and the foliage is thick and green, producing a magnificent landscape. December marks the beginning of the busy tourist season, as many people travel to escape the harsher winter months in their home countries. Prices for lodging and activities may be higher during this period.

Long Rainy Season (March to May): During these months, Zanzibar suffers considerable rainfall and greater humidity. While the rich greenery is a joy to behold, some activities may be limited owing to the weather conditions. This month is considered the low tourist season, and you may find more cheap rates for lodgings and activities.

Short Rainy Season (April to May): April and May are considered the months of the short rainy season, however the weather is often drier than the lengthy rainy season. If you want a quieter and less crowded experience, this can be a nice time to come, since visitor numbers tend to be lower.

Ultimately, the best time to visit Zanzibar depends on your interests and goals. If you want to enjoy dry and sunny weather with a wealth of activities to choose from, try going during the dry season from June to October. However, if you like a greener environment and don't mind periodic showers, the shoulder season from November to December can be more ideal. For budget-conscious tourists wanting fewer people, the extended rainy season from March to May gives an opportunity to explore Zanzibar at a more slower pace.

Visa and Requirements

As of my last knowledge update in September 2021, the visa requirements for Zanzibar could still be subject to change, so it's crucial to verify the latest information with the relevant authorities or the Tanzanian embassy or consulate in your country before organizing your trip. However, I can offer you with some broad recommendations that were current at the time of my previous update:

Visa Requirements: Most international travelers heading to Zanzibar will require a visa to enter Tanzania. Zanzibar is part of Tanzania, and the visa procedures are the same for both. The sort of visa you need depends depend on your nationality and the purpose of your travel (e.g., tourist, business, or transit).

Visa Types: Tanzania normally grants single-entry and multiple-entry visas. Single-entry visas are valid for a set term and allow you to enter Tanzania once. repeated-entry visas are frequently awarded for commercial purposes and allowing repeated entrances into the nation within a certain duration.

Visa Application: You may apply for a Tanzanian visa through Tanzanian embassies or consulates in your native country. Some nations can be eligible for getting a visa on arrival at key entry points in Tanzania, including Zanzibar International Airport and seaports. However, it's necessary to determine if this option is accessible for your nationality and the precise visa you want.

Visa Validity: Visa validity periods may vary dependent on the kind of visa issued. Tourist visas are frequently issued for visits ranging from 30 to 90 days, although again, this may vary based on your nationality.

Passport Validity: Ensure that your passport is valid for at least six months beyond your scheduled departure date from Tanzania.

Yellow Fever Vaccination: Some passengers may need to provide a valid yellow fever vaccination certificate upon arrival. Check the Tanzanian government's health regulations and recommendations for your nationality.

Supporting Documents: You could be required to supply extra documents such as a return airline ticket, proof of lodging, or evidence of adequate cash for your stay.

Please note that visa restrictions and procedures are subject to change, so it's vital to verify the latest information with the proper authorities before making any travel preparations. The Tanzanian embassy or consulate in your country will be the most dependable source for up-to-date visa information for your nationality.

Budgeting and Currency

When planning for a vacation to Zanzibar, it's vital to consider numerous elements, such as lodging, transportation, food, activities, and incidental charges. Here are some crucial considerations to bear in mind:

Accommodation: Accommodation expenses might vary greatly, depending on the sort of hotel you pick. Options range from affordable guesthouses and hostels to upscale resorts. Research and compare costs in advance to discover lodging that meets your budget and tastes.

Transportation: Local transportation prices in Zanzibar may be reasonably low. You may take public transport, such as dala-dalas (minibusses), to move about the island at a lesser rate. Taxis are also available, however they may be more expensive, especially for longer distances.

cuisine: Zanzibar provides a varied selection of dining alternatives, from affordable street cuisine to sophisticated restaurants. Local cafes and shops provide great and budget-friendly delicacies, including Swahili cuisine and fresh fish.

Activities: The cost of activities in Zanzibar might vary, depending on what you want to do. Beach activities including snorkeling, diving, and water sports may have related expenses. Entrance costs to historical places and attractions should also be addressed.

Miscellaneous Expenses: Don't forget to account for additional expenses like souvenirs, tips, and any unforeseen charges that may emerge during your vacation.

Currency: The official currency of Zanzibar, as well as Tanzania, is the Tanzanian Shilling (TZS). While certain big tourist facilities could take major international currencies like the US Dollar or the Euro, it is suggested to utilize the local currency for most purchases to avoid unfavorable exchange rates.

ATMs are accessible in bigger communities, including Stone Town, and major credit cards are accepted at select expensive places. However, it's a good idea to carry some cash, especially in smaller towns and isolated places, where cash could be the primary payment option.

Before your travel, verify with your bank about the availability of ATMs that accept foreign cards and any potential costs for international transactions. Also, advise your bank about your vacation intentions to avoid any complications with using your cards overseas.

To obtain a better idea of your budget, investigate the current currency rates and determine how much money you will need for your estimated costs during your time in Zanzibar. It's usually a good idea to carry a little extra for emergencies or unexpected .

CHAPTER 3: GETTING TO ZANZIBAR

Airports and Transportation

Zanzibar has one primary international airport and various transit alternatives to go around the island. Here's a rundown of the airports and transportation accessible in Zanzibar:

AZanzibar has one primary international airport and various transit alternatives to go around the island. Here's a rundown of the airports and transportation accessible in Zanzibar:

Airport:

Abeid Amani Karume International Airport (ZNZ): Located in Stone Town, this is the major international airport serving Zanzibar. It is well-connected to many places in Africa and several foreign cities. Many travelers come at this airport to start their Zanzibar trip.

Transportation Options:

Taxi: Taxis are accessible at the airport and in major towns. They offer a handy and pleasant method to go around the island, although they might be significantly more expensive than other choices. Negotiate the fare before commencing your journey.

Dala-dalas: Dala-dalas are the major means of public transportation in Zanzibar. These are minivans or small buses that operate on regular routes, linking large towns and villages. They are the most affordable method to travel, but they can grow crowded and may not keep to rigid timetables.

Private Car rent: You may rent private cars or drivers to tour the island at your own speed. This option gives greater freedom and comfort, especially if you want to visit off-the-beaten-path sites or take day trips to numerous sights.

Motorbike Taxi (Boda-boda): In select regions, you could encounter motorbike taxis, also known as boda-bodas. They offer a speedier method to navigate through traffic and reach spots that larger vehicles would struggle to access.

Rental vehicles: If you prefer the freedom to explore on your own, rental vehicles are available in Stone Town and at the airport. However, keep in mind that driving in Zanzibar may be problematic owing to small roads and indigenous driving customs.

Walking: In Stone Town and several smaller towns, walking is a terrific way to see the local landmarks and immerse yourself in the culture. The small lanes of Stone Town are best explored on foot.

Remember to consider your budget, comfort level, and desired level of independence while picking transportation alternatives in Zanzibar. While dala-dalas give a genuine local experience, private vehicle hire or taxis may provide better convenience and comfort for specific excursions.

Sea and Ferry Travel

Sea & Ferry Travel in Zanzibar

Zanzibar, a picturesque archipelago off the coast of East Africa, is famed for its gorgeous beaches, turquoise seas, and colorful culture. To visit this exquisite destination, sea and boat travel serve as popular and accessible modes of transportation.

boat Travel: The Zanzibar Archipelago is well-connected through its boat services, providing crucial connectivity between the islands and mainland Tanzania. The principal ferry route connects Stone Town, Zanzibar's capital, with Dar es Salaam, Tanzania's largest city. The cruise provides stunning views of the Indian Ocean and normally takes roughly two hours. The ferries are pleasant and moderately priced, making them a preferred alternative for both locals and visitors alike.

Island Hopping: For those wanting a more immersed experience, island hopping is a terrific alternative. Several smaller islands near Zanzibar, like as Pemba and Mafia, may be readily accessible by boat. Each island offers its distinct beauty, from Pemba's beautiful green sceneries to Mafia's amazing marine life, making island hopping an adventure of a lifetime.

Dhow Cruises: For a bit of genuine Zanzibari culture, embark on a dhow boat. These historic sailing vessels are a reminder of the island's maritime heritage. Sail around the shoreline, delighting in the soft sea wind as you view the gorgeous sunset over the horizon. Dhow tours typically feature snorkeling or diving possibilities, allowing a chance to experience Zanzibar's flourishing underwater ecosystem.

Diving & Snorkeling: Zanzibar is a diver's paradise with its stunning coral reefs and an assortment of marine animals. The clean, mild waters make it a perfect place for both novices and expert divers. Numerous diving centers and snorkeling trips cater to guests wanting to experience the diverse marine ecology and swim with colorful fish and unique aquatic critters.

Safety Considerations: While water travel in Zanzibar is typically safe and pleasurable, it's necessary to be careful of weather conditions and hire trustworthy operators. During the rainy season, sea conditions can become unpredictable, disrupting ferry schedules and boat cruises. Always emphasize safety and follow the counsel of qualified specialists.

In conclusion, sea and boat transport in Zanzibar give a lovely opportunity to discover the region's natural beauty and rich cultural legacy. Whether you're hopping between islands, travelling aboard a dhow, or diving into the depths, the experience offers amazing memories in this slice of paradise on the Indian Ocean .

CHAPTER 4: ISLAND EXPLORATION

Unveiling Stone Town's Charms

As you enter into the heart of Zanzibar, the old maze-like streets and antique structures of Stone Town welcome you with open arms. This UNESCO World Heritage Site, located on the western coast of Zanzibar, is a treasure mine of history and culture ready to be discovered.

History and Architecture: Stone Town's rich history is obvious as you travel through its convoluted alleyways. Influenced by a combination of Arab, Persian, Indian, and European civilizations, the town's architecture shows a unique blend of influences. The delicately carved wooden doors, magnificent balconies, and formidable strongholds are reminders of a bygone period. Visit the Old Fort, a 17th-century fortification that originally functioned as a bulwark against Portuguese invasion and subsequently turned into a cultural center.

Spice Markets and Delights: Zanzibar's moniker, the "Spice Island," stems from its rich spice trading history. Explore the busy marketplaces packed with a plethora of exotic spices such as cloves, nutmeg, cinnamon, and cardamom. Engage with friendly merchants, learn about traditional spice growing, and take home aromatic mementos. Don't forget to tempt your taste buds with delectable Swahili meals at local eateries, presenting an assortment of tastes influenced by the island's spices.

The House of Wonders: A visit to the House of Wonders is a necessity to dive into Zanzibar's regal heritage. This stately edifice, originally created as the Sultan's ceremonial palace, got its moniker due to being one of the first structures on the island to receive electricity and running water. Today, it functions as a museum displaying Zanzibar's history and cultural heritage, including exhibitions of traditional items and historical relics.

Forodhani Gardens & Sunset Dhow Cruises: The gorgeous Forodhani Gardens, located along the seashore, is a fantastic area to unwind and enjoy stunning sunsets over the Indian Ocean. In the evenings, the gardens convert into a busy night market, serving great fish and local specialties. As evening comes, consider embarking on a dhow sail, viewing the sky ablaze with colours of orange and pink while being serenaded by the soft lapping of waves.

Cultural Encounters: Engage with the locals and immerse yourself in the warm hospitality of Zanzibar's population. Visit the Zanzibar Gallery and support local artists and artisans, or watch a traditional Taarab music performance, a combination of Swahili, Arab, and Indian influences, to experience the island's lively cultural life.

Beach Escapes: While discovering the beauties of Stone Town, don't forget to take a short journey to the adjacent magnificent beaches. Bask in the sun, dive into the pristine seas, or try your hand at various water activities like snorkeling, diving, and sailing.

In conclusion, exposing Stone Town's attractions is a compelling journey through history, culture, and natural beauty. This charming region of Zanzibar has a variety of experiences that will leave you with cherished recollections of an island that has weathered the test of time while embracing its lively history.

Exploring Spice Plantations

A vacation to Zanzibar wouldn't be complete without immersing yourself in the island's famed spice farms. Embark on a sensory adventure through verdant fields, where you'll meet a plethora of aromatic spices that have molded Zanzibar's history and won it the nickname "Spice Island."

Guided excursions: Numerous guided excursions are available, allowing you to visit the spice farms with expert natives who will impart their knowledge of the island's spice trade and farming traditions. They will expose you to a great assortment of spices, such as cloves, vanilla, cinnamon, cardamom, and nutmeg, among others.

Cloves - The King of Spices: Discover the significance of cloves, which have been a cornerstone of Zanzibar's economy for generations. Learn about the numerous steps of clove production, from harvesting to drying, and the crucial role this spice has had in defining the island's history and culture.

Vanilla Orchids: Witness the lovely vanilla orchids, which yield one of the world's most loved and costly spices. Delve into the complicated process of hand-pollinating vanilla blooms and the significant labor necessary to create this highly-prized spice.

Cinnamon and Cardamom: Unearth the secrets underlying the production of cinnamon and cardamom. Marvel at the sight of cinnamon trees and hear how cardamom pods are meticulously plucked to ensure their particular flavor and perfume.

Interactive Experience: Many spice farms provide a hands-on experience, enabling you to touch, smell, and taste the numerous spices right from the source. Savor the powerful smell of freshly crushed cloves or the sweet perfume of cinnamon, opening your senses to the beauties of nature.

Traditional food: During your tour to the spice plantations, indulge on traditional Swahili food laced with the island's fragrant spices. Enjoy a tasty lunch with meals seasoned with the exact spices you've tasted during your tour.

Souvenir Shopping: Before waving farewell to the spice farms, seize the chance to purchase high-quality spices to bring home with you. These original Zanzibari spices make for fantastic presents or complements to your culinary pursuits, delivering a sense of Zanzibar long after your visit.

Community and Sustainability: Some spice farms also promote sustainable agricultural techniques and benefit local communities. By participating in these trips, you help to the preservation of traditional knowledge and sustainable livelihoods for local farmers.

In conclusion, seeing the spice farms of Zanzibar gives a delightful glimpse into the island's history, culture, and olfactory riches. The event is a celebration of nature's treasures and a monument to the ongoing fascination of the Spice Island.

Sun, Sand, and Sea on the Beaches

Zanzibar's picture-perfect beaches lure vacationers with their pristine shoreline, turquoise oceans, and plentiful sunshine. A coastal paradise tucked in the Indian Ocean, the island provides a lovely vacation for beach lovers seeking leisure and adventure.

Powdery White Sands: Sink your toes into the smooth, powdery sands that border Zanzibar's shoreline. From famous places like Nungwi and Kendwa to quieter treasures like Paje and Matemwe, each beach has its particular character, giving adequate room for relaxing, beach activities, or calm strolls along the shore.

Azure Waters and Marine Life: Dip into the appealing azure waters that are delightfully warm throughout the year. Snorkeling fans will be pleased by the vivid coral reefs abounding with colorful fish and marine life. The island's seas also give fantastic prospects for scuba diving, where you may see gorgeous sea turtles, lively dolphins, and even majestic whale sharks in their native habitat.

Dhow Cruises & Sailing Adventures: Sail through the glittering seas aboard traditional dhows, a symbol of Zanzibar's nautical heritage. These wooden sailing boats provide unique sunset excursions and island-hopping adventures, allowing you to explore neighboring islands and sandbanks.

Water Sports Galore: Thrill-seekers may enjoy in an assortment of water sports. Try kite surfing at Paje, where the continuous breeze and shallow waves provide perfect conditions for beginners and specialists alike. Jet skiing, parasailing, and water skiing are all offered for those wanting an adrenaline rush.

Spectacular Sunsets: As the sun begins to drop over the Indian Ocean, Zanzibar's beaches turn into breathtaking settings. Witness beautiful sunsets, painting the sky with colours of pink, orange, and purple, providing for a fantastic background for romantic moments or evening beach picnics.

seaside Dining: Relish in a fantastic gastronomic experience by dining at the various seaside restaurants and pubs. Savor freshly caught seafood and delight in unique beverages while listening to the calm lapping of waves.

Beach Bonfires and Full Moon Parties: Experience the bustling nightlife on the beaches of Zanzibar. Gather around beach bonfires, where residents and visitors alike gather together for drumming sessions, dancing, and storytelling. During full moon evenings, exciting gatherings take place under the starlit sky, generating an atmosphere of joy and friendship.

Wellness & Serenity: Unwind and refresh at one of the island's beachside resorts providing spa treatments and yoga classes. The calming sound of the waves and the mild sea wind create a quiet ambience, suitable for relaxation and reflection.

In conclusion, Zanzibar's beaches provide an exquisite combination of leisure, adventure, and natural beauty. Whether you desire to bask in the sun, discover the undersea marvels, or just revel in the island's coastline charms, the beaches of Zanzibar guarantee a memorable and exquisite retreat.

Wildlife Encounters on Chumbe Island

Chumbe Island, located just off the coast of Zanzibar, is a beautiful tropical refuge that captivates tourists with its rich biodiversity and protected marine habitat. As a protected marine reserve, this little island provides unique opportunity for wildlife encounters and eco-adventures.

Coral Reefs and Marine Life: The coral reefs around Chumbe Island are a treasure trove of marine life. Snorkel or dive into the crystal-clear waters to find a kaleidoscope of vivid corals and an abundance of fish species. From colorful parrotfish and angelfish to elegant rays and sea turtles, the underwater environment here is a haven for marine biodiversity.

Chumbe Forest Reserve: Beyond the beaches and coral reefs, Chumbe Island is home to a unique and protected coral rag forest. Take guided nature excursions in this deep woodland to observe various birds, including rare species like the Pemba Sunbird. Spot the rare coconut crabs, the biggest terrestrial arthropods on world, who move freely in the jungle.

Chumbe's Coral Rag caverns: Explore the intriguing coral rag caverns on Chumbe Island. These old limestone caverns harbor a mysterious ambiance and give sanctuary to a variety of bats and other nocturnal critters. Guided cave excursions give insights into the island's geology and the species that live these beneath rooms.

Chumbe Island's Giant Coconut Crab Conservation: Chumbe Island is a refuge for the endangered giant coconut crab. With their distinctive look and incredible size, these crabs are a fascinating sight. Through conservation efforts, the island protects the protection of these amazing species and helps to their population's maintenance.

Turtle Nesting Season: Chumbe Island plays a significant role in sea turtle conservation. From November through February, the island's beaches become nesting locations for green and hawksbill turtles. Witnessing these amazing animals coming ashore to deposit their eggs is a genuinely awe-inspiring event, underlining the significance of safeguarding their habitats.

Eco-friendly Accommodation: The Chumbe Island Coral Park is a sustainable eco-lodge that offers a unique and responsible approach to enjoy the island's animals and natural beauties. The eco-lodge's design and procedures promote environmental protection and minimum influence on the island's sensitive ecosystem.

Education and Awareness: Chumbe Island is not simply a refuge for animals but also an educational centre for tourists. The Chumbe Island Coral Park team conducts seminars and awareness programs to emphasize the relevance of conservation efforts and the importance of conserving the island's unique biodiversity.

In conclusion, Chumbe Island's animal encounters give a rare opportunity to engage with nature in a pure and protected location. This eco-paradise serves as an example for sustainable tourism and stands as a monument to the necessity of protecting vulnerable ecosystems for future generations to love and learn from.

CHAPTER 5: ZANZIBAR'S CULTURE AND TRADITIONS

Festivals and Celebrations

Zanzibar's dynamic culture is vividly represented in its myriad festivals and festivities, when people and visitors join together to delight in customs, music, dance, and religious events. These bustling events give a unique opportunity to immerse yourself in the island's rich past and feel the essence of Zanzibar.

1. Zanzibar International Film Festival (ZIFF): As one of Africa's most famous film festivals, ZIFF exhibits a varied selection of films from throughout the world. Held yearly in Stone Town, this event promotes African cinema, fostering cultural interchange and supporting local cinematic talent.

2. Sauti za Busara Music Festival: This dynamic music festival brings together an assortment of performers from Africa and beyond to present a colorful combination of traditional and modern music. Held in Stone Town, Sauti za

Busara delivers a stunning presentation of East African rhythms and songs.

3. Mwaka Kogwa Festival: This distinctive Shirazi New Year event takes place in Makunduchi hamlet. The festival incorporates ancient traditions, such as mock fights, when people playfully resolve issues from the past year and welcome the new year with pleasure and friendship.

4. Eid al-Fitr and Eid al-Adha: As prominent Islamic festivals, Eid al-Fitr and Eid al-Adha are cheerfully celebrated across Zanzibar. Locals dress in their nicest apparel, attend special prayers, and have celebratory feasts with family and friends, creating a sense of camaraderie and harmony.

5. Revolution Day (Mapinduzi Day): On January 12th, Zanzibar celebrates the Zanzibar Revolution of 1964, which led to the collapse of the Sultanate and the formation of the People's Republic of Zanzibar. Festivities include parades, cultural performances, and numerous events to celebrate the island's heritage.

6. Mwaka Mpya Festival: As part of the Swahili New Year festival, villagers congregate on the beach to observe the first appearance of the new moon. Drumming, singing, and traditional dances fill the air as people join together to welcome the new year with optimism and hope.

7. Bullfighting (Ngoma): A unique show in Zanzibar's culture, bullfighting activities take place in communities around the island. Unlike traditional bullfights, no damage is given to the animals. Instead, bulls are driven to lock horns and exhibit their strength as onlookers cheer on.

8. Jamboree Festival: Celebrated in the village of Dole, the Jamboree Festival emphasizes local cultural acts, including taarab music, dance, and poetry. The festival emphasizes cultural preservation and appreciation while building a sense of pride in Zanzibari customs.

In conclusion, Zanzibar's festivals and festivities are a monument to the island's unique cultural past and the genuine hospitality of its people. From film and music festivals to religious and traditional festivities, each occasion gives a magnificent opportunity to enjoy life and embrace the variety that distinguishes this fascinating corner of the globe.

Art and Handicrafts

Zanzibar offers a rich creative legacy that is elegantly portrayed via its traditional handicrafts and modern art scene. From delicate woodcarvings to vivid paintings, the island's creative offerings demonstrate the ingenuity and cultural variety of its inhabitants.

Woodcarvings: Woodcarving is a major form of creative expression in Zanzibar. Skilled artisans make finely carved doors, furniture, and ornamental things. The wooden doors, embellished with beautiful geometric patterns and precise motifs, are notably recognized for their workmanship and historical value.

Kangas and Kitenges: Kangas and kitenges are vividly colored textiles embellished with Swahili proverbs, patterns, and vibrant motifs. These adaptable fabrics are utilized as garments, headscarves, and ornamental elements. The vibrant fabrics represent the island's vivacious personality and are appreciated by both natives and visitors alike.

Tinga Tinga Paintings: Inspired by traditional African art, Tinga Tinga paintings are a bright and contemporary form of expression. Created using brilliant colors and intricate patterns, these paintings generally portray images from nature, animals, and local life, giving a bit of Zanzibar's creative flare to any room.

Copper Crafts: Copper crafts are another remarkable feature of Zanzibar's craftsmanship. Skilled artists produce stunning jewelry, decorations, and ornamental objects utilizing the age-old method of copper embossing. These handcrafted artifacts highlight the island's expertise and devotion to maintaining traditional crafts.

Baskets and Weaving: Basketry and weaving are vital components of Zanzibar's traditional history. Talented weavers masterfully produce baskets, mats, and household goods from natural fibers, exhibiting a blend of beauty and usefulness.

Makonde Carvings: The Makonde people of Zanzibar are known for their complex wood carvings, notably their creative portrayals of abstract creatures and human forms. These carvings frequently hold rich cultural and symbolic connotations, reflecting pieces of local customs and mythology.

Art Galleries and Studios: Zanzibar's lively art culture is mirrored in many galleries and studios around the island. Art fans may discover current works by local and international artists, offering a look into the growing creative environment of Zanzibar.

Art and Cultural Festivals: Zanzibar also organizes art and cultural festivals that promote local artistic ability. These events give opportunity for artists to present their works, share ideas, and encourage creative partnerships.

Supporting Local Artisans: Visitors may assist Zanzibar's art and handicraft community by purchasing locally-made crafts and artworks. Shopping at local markets and supporting craftsmen directly contributes to the preservation of traditional crafts and the livelihoods of local people.

In conclusion, Zanzibar's art and handicrafts show a blend of heritage and contemporary expression. The island's cultural offerings exhibit the beauty of Swahili culture, the talent of local artists, and the vibrant spirit that permeates every part of life on this wonderful island.

Culinary Delights

Zanzibar's culinary pleasures provide a delectable combination of tastes influenced by the island's rich cultural heritage and spice trade history. From delectable seafood meals to fragrant spices and Swahili delicacies, the island's cuisine is a pleasant voyage for the taste senses.

1. Zanzibari Seafood: With its closeness to the Indian Ocean, Zanzibar is a heaven for seafood lovers. Indulge in fresh catches of fish, prawns, lobsters, and calamari cooked with local seasonings and grilled to perfection. The combination of spices complements the natural tastes, making every meal a wonderful feast.

2. Pilau Rice: Pilau rice is a favorite Zanzibari meal, commonly eaten during special events and festivals. This fragrant rice dish is laced with a variety of spices including cloves, cinnamon, and cardamom, creating a delicious and aromatic mixture of tastes.

3. Zanzibari Pizza (Urojo): Zanzibari pizza, called locally as urojo, is a unique and excellent street snack. It comprises of a crispy crepe-like dough filled with various toppings such as minced meat, veggies, eggs, and cheese, then folded and roasted to perfection.

4. Coconut-based recipes: Coconut is a major component in Zanzibari cuisine, and you'll find it employed in many recipes. From coconut curries to coconut chutneys and coconut milk-based sauces, the tropical fruit offers a creamy and unique touch to many Zanzibari pleasures.

5. Zanzibari Snacks (Mahindi ya Nazi): Mahindi ya nazi, or coconut corn on the cob, is a popular snack found on the streets of Zanzibar. The maize is simmered in coconut milk and served with a dusting of spices, creating a great balance of sweet and spicy tastes.

6. Swahili Tea and Coffee: Indulge in the authentic Swahili tea and coffee experience. Swahili tea is a rich spiced tea, commonly savored with milk and sugar, while Swahili coffee is dark and fragrant, delivering a delicious pick-me-up.

7. Zanzibari Sweets (Mandazi and Kaimati): Mandazi, a sweet and fluffy fried dough, and kaimati, miniature golden dumplings steeped in sugar syrup, are popular Zanzibari sweets commonly eaten as morning treats or afternoon snacks.

8. Exotic Fruits: Zanzibar features a plethora of tropical fruits, including mangoes, pineapples, jackfruits, and bananas. Savor the richness and juiciness of these fruits, commonly served as fresh fruit platters or in fruit salads.

9. Spice Tours and Cooking Classes: To truly experience Zanzibar's culinary pleasures, try joining a spice tour to

learn about the island's famed spices and their application in local recipes. Additionally, culinary lessons provide the chance to acquire original recipes and skills from local chefs.

In conclusion, Zanzibar's culinary pleasures are a combination of exquisite tastes that represent the island's numerous cultural influences and plentiful natural resources. From seafood feasts to fragrant spices and sweet delights, the island's cuisine is a feast for both the senses and the spirit.

CHAPTER 6: ADVENTURE ACTIVITIES

Diving and Snorkeling

Diving and snorkeling in Zanzibar give remarkable opportunity to explore the island's lively underwater environment and observe the splendor of its coral reefs and marine life. With clean seas, various marine animals, and experienced dive operators, Zanzibar is a diver's paradise.

Diving in Zanzibar: Zanzibar provides a variety of dive sites ideal for both beginners and expert divers. The island's coral reefs are alive with colorful marine life, including tropical fish, rays, moray eels, and turtles. For more brave divers, there are possibilities to encounter bigger wildlife such as reef sharks and dolphins. Some significant diving spots are Mnemba Atoll, Leven Bank, and Kichwani Reef.

Snorkeling in Zanzibar: Snorkeling is equally gratifying in Zanzibar, making it an accessible pastime for all ages and experience levels. Many snorkeling areas may be accessible straight from the shore, affording sights of colourful coral gardens and a diversity of fish species. Mnemba Atoll, with its crystal-clear waters, is a favorite place for snorkelers to study marine life up close.

Turtle Sanctuary: Visitors may also get a unique experience by snorkeling with sea turtles in the Mnarani Marine Turtle Conservation Pond. This refuge provides as a protected environment for wounded or stranded turtles before they are released back into the wild.

Dolphin Tours: For an exciting encounter, try taking a dolphin tour at Kizimkazi. These tours provide the possibility to view bottlenose and humpback dolphins in their natural surroundings. However, it's necessary to prioritize appropriate tourist activities and prevent upsetting the animals.

Night Dives: Experienced divers might choose for night dives to view the underwater world in a new light. Night dives show unique nocturnal marine animals, as well as the stunning bioluminescence of some organisms.

Dive facilities and Operators: Zanzibar features various dive facilities and operators that comply to safety requirements and sustainable diving methods. Whether you're a newbie or an expert diver, competent guides and instructors are available to ensure a safe and fun diving experience.

Conservation projects: Many diving operators in Zanzibar are actively interested in marine conservation projects. They encourage appropriate diving techniques, run reef conservation initiatives, and teach divers about the necessity of protecting the delicate marine habitat.

In conclusion, diving and snorkeling in Zanzibar give a look into the enchanting underwater environment of the Indian Ocean. The island's beautiful reefs, rich marine life, and devotion to conservation make it a riveting destination for water enthusiasts and environment lovers alike.

Sailing and Dhow Cruises

Sailing and dhow tours are classic activities in Zanzibar, giving a romantic and scenic opportunity to explore the island's stunning shoreline and pure waterways. These historic wooden sailing boats, known as dhows, have been a vital part of Zanzibar's nautical legacy for decades, giving a genuine and fascinating trip.

Dhow Cruises: Dhow cruises are a must-do activity in Zanzibar, allowing an opportunity to travel around the Indian Ocean's shimmering seas and experience breathtaking views of the island's shoreline. Sunset dhow excursions are particularly popular, as they give a wonderful experience of viewing the sky painted with colours of orange and pink as the sun drops below the horizon.

Island Hopping: Dhows are frequently employed for island-hopping trips, carrying passengers to surrounding islands and sandbanks. These quiet areas, generally surrounded by crystal-clear seas, are great for snorkeling, swimming, and resting on private beaches.

Fishing cruises: For those wanting a genuine fishing experience, dhow fishing cruises are offered, allowing the chance to try your hand at traditional Zanzibari fishing tactics. Catching fish using age-old ways with expert local fisherman is a memorable and gratifying sport.

Dolphin excursions: Dhow cruises in Kizimkazi typically incorporate dolphin excursions, allowing you to observe playful bottlenose and humpback dolphins in their natural habitat. However, it's vital to emphasize the well-being of these aquatic species and avoid upsetting them throughout the visits.

Sunset and Moonlight meals: Dhow cruises can also be accompanied with romantic meals. Relish a great seafood supper on board while you watch the sun lowering over the water, creating an exquisite ambiance. Some operators even provide moonlight dinner cruises, delivering a unique dining experience beneath the starry night sky.

Sailing Regattas: Throughout the year, Zanzibar holds sailing regattas that draw both locals and foreign sailors. These festivities reflect the island's maritime history and provide an exciting spectacle for viewers to experience the elegance and beauty of traditional dhows in action.

Private Charters and occasions: Dhows can be privately rented for special occasions like weddings, birthdays, or business parties. This customised experience allows you to tailor the trip according to your tastes, making it a memorable and unique occasion.

In conclusion, sailing and dhow tours in Zanzibar provide a taste of the island's nautical traditions and the ability to immerse yourself in the stunning splendor of the Indian Ocean. Whether you select for a peaceful sunset cruise or an exciting island-hopping trip, the experience ensures an exquisite and unique ride on the serene seas of Zanzibar.

Trekking and Hiking

While Zanzibar is famed for its magnificent beaches and marine adventures, the island also provides possibilities for climbing and hiking, allowing an opportunity to explore its lush landscapes and natural treasures.

Jozani Forest trip: Embark on a trip through the Jozani Forest, Zanzibar's sole national park and a UNESCO-recognized conservation area. This tropical jungle is home to the endangered red colobus monkey, a species found exclusively on the island. Guided excursions lead you into the deep foliage, allowing you to view these playful primates and other animals, such as Sykes' monkeys and other bird species.

Masingini Forest Trek: The Masingini Forest Reserve is another place perfect for trekking. It provides a calm atmosphere, with ancient trees, meandering walkways, and a broad diversity of flora and wildlife. As you wander through this natural reserve, you may see several endemic bird species and small creatures.

Ngezi Forest Reserve Hike: On Pemba Island, the Ngezi Forest Reserve gives a fantastic hiking option. The reserve has unusual plant species and a tranquil ambiance, making it a pleasant area to explore. Keep a watch out for the Pemba flying fox, one of the world's biggest bat species, which may be seen resting in the forest.

Mangrove Forest Exploration: Mangrove forests border areas of Zanzibar's coastline, producing a complex network of waterways. Guided tours into these mangrove habitats give insights into their critical function in maintaining marine life, acting as nursery for many marine species.

Prison Island Hike: On Prison Island (also known as Changuu Island), a hike up the hill affords panoramic views of the ocean and the neighboring islands. The island is also home to a colony of huge Aldabra tortoises, which you may encounter during your stay.

Sunrise or Sunset Hikes: Hiking to elevation areas, such as views or hilltops, allows you to see spectacular sunrises or sunsets over the Indian Ocean. These amazing events provide unforgettable memories and photo possibilities.

Off-the-Beaten-road paths: While touring the islands, try wandering off the beaten road to uncover secret paths and unknown places. Local guides may frequently direct you to lesser-known areas with pristine vistas and a true impression of the island's natural splendor.

In conclusion, trekking and climbing in Zanzibar give a distinct view of the island's beauty, away from the beaches and coastal vistas. Whether exploring lush woods, viewing animals, or seeing breathtaking sunrises and sunsets, these activities enable you to connect with nature and enjoy the different landscapes that Zanzibar has to offer.

CHAPTER 7: SUSTAINABLE TRAVEL IN ZANZIBAR

Responsible Tourism initiatives

Responsible tourism projects in Zanzibar strive to encourage sustainable practices that benefit the environment, local populations, and cultural heritage. These activities are vital to conserving the island's natural beauty and guaranteeing its long-term survival as a tourist destination. Here are some significant responsible tourism efforts in Zanzibar:

1. Marine Conservation and Reef Protection: Various organizations and diving operators in Zanzibar actively participate in marine conservation activities. They do reef cleanups, encourage proper diving techniques, and increase awareness about the vulnerable coral reefs and marine ecosystems. Responsible tourists are asked not to touch or harm corals and marine life during snorkeling and diving activities.

2. trash Management and Recycling: Responsible tourism efforts stress effective trash management and recycling procedures. Hotels, resorts, and local businesses seek to eliminate single-use plastic and encourage guests to use reusable water bottles. Waste sorting and recycling processes are being introduced to reduce the environmental effect.

3. Supporting Local Communities: Responsible tourism encourages travelers to support local communities by buying locally manufactured handicrafts, products, and services. This method generates economic empowerment and sustainable livelihoods for the island's population.

4. Cultural Preservation and Respect: Visitors are asked to respect local customs, traditions, and cultural practices. Responsible tourism projects foster cultural understanding and sensitivity, encouraging guests to participate in cultural experiences with respect for local values and beliefs.

5. Wildlife Protection: Efforts are made to safeguard and conserve the distinctive wildlife of Zanzibar, including the endangered red colobus monkey and huge Aldabra tortoises. Responsible tourism methods focus on seeing

wildlife from a distance and avoiding any behaviors that may disrupt or injure the animals.

6. Sustainable Accommodations: Many hotels and resorts in Zanzibar have embraced sustainability concepts. They employ energy-saving measures, help local communities, and engage in eco-friendly initiatives such as water conservation and trash reduction.

7. Community-Based Tourism: Community-based tourism programs give chances for travelers to connect directly with local communities. This allows people to experience real cultural encounters while contributing directly to the well-being of the communities they visit.

8. Supporting Conservation groups: Responsible travelers may help numerous conservation groups and projects that strive towards protecting Zanzibar's natural and cultural heritage. Donations and volunteering opportunities with trustworthy organizations may make a major influence on conservation efforts.

9. Eco-Friendly Activities and Tours: Many tour companies in Zanzibar provide eco-friendly tours and activities that

stress minimal environmental effect. This includes low-impact water sports, nature hikes, and other activities that respect the natural environment.

In conclusion, responsible tourism initiatives play a critical role in maintaining the sustainable growth of Zanzibar's tourism sector. By encouraging environmental protection, helping local communities, and safeguarding cultural legacy, responsible tourists may contribute positively to the well-being of Zanzibar and its people for years to come.

Supporting Local Communities

Supporting local communities in Zanzibar is a meaningful and responsible approach to make a positive influence during your stay. Here are some ways you may help local communities and contribute to their well-being:

1. Shopping Local: Purchase locally created items and handicrafts directly from local craftsmen and dealers. By doing so, you support their livelihoods and help conserve traditional crafts and cultural heritage.

2. Dining at Local Restaurants: Opt for dining at local eateries and street food vendors that provide typical Zanzibari delicacies. This not only supports local companies but also gives a genuine gastronomic experience.

3. Hiring Local Guides and Services: Choose local guides and operators for tours and activities. They hold vital expertise about the area and contribute to the local economy.

4. Staying at Community-Based Accommodations: Consider staying at community-based lodges or guesthouses that

contribute back to the local community. These lodgings generally support community programs and activities, helping the people in the region.

5. Engaging in Responsible Tourism Activities: Participate in responsible tourism activities that include local communities, such as visiting local schools or community centers, watching cultural performances, or taking part in local festivals.

6. Learning About Local Culture: Take the time to learn about the local culture, customs, and traditions. Show respect for their way of life and communicate with the locals in a sensitive and culturally acceptable manner.

7. Giving Back Through working: If you have the time and abilities, try working with trustworthy groups that promote community development projects. Volunteering may be a meaningful method to directly contribute to the community's well-being.

8. Supporting Social firms: Look for social firms in Zanzibar that are focused on having beneficial social and

environmental effect. These firms generally reinvest their income into community development projects.

9. Responsible Souvenir Shopping: When buying souvenirs, consider things that are responsibly sourced and made. Avoid purchasing things created from endangered species or materials that harm the environment.

10. giving to Local Causes: If you want to make a direct contribution, try giving to local charities or community programs that address vital concerns such as education, healthcare, or environmental protection.

In conclusion, helping local communities in Zanzibar is a meaningful approach to enhance your holiday experience while making a significant difference. By choosing to connect with local businesses, honoring cultural values, and contributing to community development initiatives, you may make a lasting, good influence on the lives of the people you encounter throughout your journey.

CHAPTER 8:DAY TRIPS AND EXCURSIONS

Prison Land and Giant Tortoises

Prison Land:

Prison Island, also known as Changuu Island, is a tiny and attractive island located off the coast of Stone Town, Zanzibar. Despite its name, the island was never really utilized as a jail. Instead, it was initially designed to function as a quarantine post for African slaves. Later on, it was modified into a jail, but it was rarely utilized for that purpose.

Today, Prison Island is a renowned tourist site, particularly noted for its huge Aldabra tortoises. These gorgeous creatures were a gift from the Seychelles government, and they have flourished on the island. The Aldabra tortoises are among the biggest tortoise species in the world and may live for over a century.

Visitors to Prison Island have the rare chance to get up close and personal with these gentle giants. The tortoises walk freely over the island, and visitors may feed them and even get the chance to touch them under the supervision of the local guides.

Apart from the enormous tortoises, Prison Island also boasts magnificent beaches and crystal-clear seas, making it a perfect site for swimming, snorkeling, and resting in a calm setting. Exploring the island's old structures and learning about its status as a quarantine station adds an added dimension of mystery to the visit.

As part of responsible tourism activities, it's necessary for tourists to treat the island and its species with respect and care. Following the criteria provided by the local government and tour companies guarantees that the tortoises and their environment are safeguarded and conserved for future generations to enjoy.

Giant Tortoises:

Giant tortoises are a fascinating species recognized for their extraordinary size and endurance. In Zanzibar, notably on Prison Island (Changuu Island), you may encounter the Aldabra giant tortoises (Aldabrachelys gigantea), which are among the biggest tortoises in the world.

The Aldabra tortoises are endemic to the Aldabra Atoll in the Seychelles and were sent to Prison Island as a gift from the Seychelles government. These gentle giants have flourished on the island and have become one of the primary attractions for tourists visiting Zanzibar.

Aldabra tortoises are herbivorous reptiles and primarily graze on plants, including grasses, leaves, and fruits. They are recognized for their calm and steady motions, and their shell can function as a shield, giving protection from possible predators in their habitat.

One of the noteworthy aspects of the Aldabra tortoises is their extraordinary lifetime. They may live for far over a century, with some people known to have reached ages exceeding 200 years.

Visiting Prison Island gives a rare opportunity to engage with these wonderful creatures up close. The tortoises walk freely on the island, and travelers may feed them and study their behavior while being accompanied by skilled local workers who safeguard the well-being of the creatures.

As with any wildlife interaction, it's vital to respect the guidelines provided by the local government and tour companies to safeguard the safety and conservation of the tortoises and their natural environment. Responsible tourist practices are vital to safeguard these wonderful species and maintain their existence for future generations to admire and enjoy.

Jozani Forest and Red Colobus Monkeys

Jozani Forest is a natural wonder found in Zanzibar and is the island's sole national park. It is a beautiful tropical forest reserve that encompasses around 50 square kilometers, allowing visitors an opportunity to explore the island's distinctive flora and animals. One of the attractions of the Jozani Forest is the ability to observe the endangered Zanzibar red colobus monkeys (Piliocolobus kirkii).

Red Colobus Monkeys: The Zanzibar red colobus monkeys are a rare and endemic species found solely in the woods of Unguja, the major island of Zanzibar. They are noted for their unusual red-brown fur, contrasted with a black face, hands, and feet. These nimble and gregarious monkeys are famed for their acrobatic talents as they swing through the trees.

Conservation Significance: The red colobus monkeys in Jozani Forest are highly endangered, with a population of only roughly 2,000 individuals. Their habitat has been impacted by deforestation and human encroachment, placing them at risk. As a result, Jozani Forest plays a significant role in the conservation efforts to safeguard these monkeys and their delicate ecology.

Visiting Jozani Forest: When visiting Jozani Forest, you may join guided tours lead by skilled local guides. These trips give an opportunity to watch the red colobus monkeys in their natural environment. The guides give insights into the behavior and features of the monkeys, as well as information on the forest's rich biodiversity.

Other animals and Flora: In addition to the red colobus monkeys, Jozani Forest is home to other types of animals, including Sykes' monkeys, bushbabies, and numerous bird species. The forest is also recognized for its unique plant life, with a range of tree types, including mangroves and mahogany.

Ecological Importance: Apart from its significance for animal protection, Jozani Forest also performs a crucial ecological purpose. It works as a carbon sink, absorbing and storing carbon dioxide, which helps moderate climate change. The forest also sustains a delicate balance of habitats, contributing to the island's overall environmental health.

Responsible Tourism: As with any animal encounter, responsible tourism is necessary in Jozani Forest. Visitors should observe the guidelines given by the park officials and guides to ensure the well-being of the red colobus monkeys and the preservation of their environment. Avoid feeding the monkeys and keep a safe distance to prevent any disruption to their natural behavior.

In conclusion, Jozani Forest and its red colobus monkeys are a valued element of Zanzibar's natural heritage. A visit to this national park gives an exceptional chance to view these endangered primates in their wild and natural surroundings, while also supporting to the conservation efforts that secure their survival for years to come.

Mnemba Atoll and Marine Life

Mnemba Atoll is a tiny, private island located off the northeast coast of Zanzibar, Tanzania. It is famous for its immaculate coral reefs and colorful marine life, making it a paradise for snorkelers and scuba divers. Here's what you can expect when visiting Mnemba Atoll:

Marine Biodiversity: Mnemba Atoll is part of the protected Mnemba Island Marine Conservation Area, designed to maintain the unique marine biodiversity of the region. The waters around the atoll are filled with a broad range of marine animals, including beautiful corals, reef fish, sea turtles, dolphins, and even occasional sightings of whale sharks and humpback whales during specific seasons.

Snorkeling and Diving: Mnemba Atoll is well renowned for its superb snorkeling and diving possibilities. The shallow coral reefs are easily accessible for snorkelers, and the crystal-clear waters give great visibility to view the undersea life. Divers may explore the deeper areas of the reefs, where they can encounter a wealth of marine life, including schools of tropical fish, rays, and other invertebrates.

Coral Reefs & Conservation: The coral reefs at Mnemba Atoll are lively and robust, showing a remarkable array of hard and soft corals. Conservation initiatives, including ethical diving and snorkeling activities, have aided to maintaining these delicate ecosystems. Visitors are asked to comply to eco-friendly principles to safeguard the coral reefs and marine life.

Dolphin Watching: Mnemba Atoll is also noted for its regular dolphin sightings. Bottlenose and humpback dolphins are commonly sighted playing and swimming in the seas near the atoll. Some travel providers offer dolphin watching tours, allowing guests to observe these lively creatures in their natural surroundings.

Turtle Nesting Sites: Mnemba Atoll acts as a nesting habitat for green and hawksbill turtles. During nesting season (November to February), visitors may have the rare opportunity to observe these gorgeous creatures coming ashore to deposit their eggs. Responsible turtle monitoring methods are vital to avoid interruptions and enhance healthy nesting.

Exclusive Island Experience: Mnemba Atoll is a private island, and its exclusivity adds to its pure nature. It is home to a single luxury resort, providing visitors a calm and private experience in harmony with nature.

Responsible Tourism: Visiting Mnemba Atoll should be done carefully to preserve the protection of the delicate marine habitat. Adhering to the rules provided by the resort and local authorities, such as avoiding harming or disturbing marine life and not leaving any rubbish behind, is vital to conserving the atoll's natural beauty.

In conclusion, Mnemba Atoll is a marine wonderland that gives a great opportunity to discover the beauty and diversity of Zanzibar's underwater environment. Whether snorkeling, diving, or simply enjoying the peace of the island, a visit to Mnemba Atoll offers an extraordinary experience with the wonders of the Indian Ocean's aquatic life.

CHAPTER 9: PRACTICAL TIPS AND SAFETY

Health and Medical Information

Zanzibar, like any other location, has its distinct health and medical landscape. It's necessary for tourists and inhabitants alike to be aware of specific health precautions and medical services accessible on the island.

Health Considerations:

vaccines: Before coming to Zanzibar, it is essential to check the current travel health advice and verify that you are up-to-date on standard vaccines, as well as any supplementary immunizations necessary for the location.

Malaria: Zanzibar is considered a malaria-endemic location. Travelers are recommended to take proper anti-malarial medicine and utilize insect repellents, mosquito nets, and protective clothing to limit the risk of malaria.

Water and Food Safety: It is important to consume bottled or boiled water and avoid ingesting raw or undercooked food to prevent foodborne infections.

Sun Protection: The tropical environment of Zanzibar implies that sun protection is necessary. Use sunscreen, wear hats, and seek shade to avoid sunburn and heat-related diseases.

Hygiene: Practicing proper personal hygiene, such as regular handwashing, can help reduce the spread of infectious illnesses.

Medical Facilities:

Stone Town Hospitals: Stone Town, the capital of Zanzibar, is home to the primary medical institutions on the island. The Mnazi Mmoja Hospital and the Zanzibar Central Hospital provide emergency and general medical services.

Private Clinics: There are private clinics and health facilities in Stone Town and other large towns, offering a range of medical services to locals and visitors.

Pharmacies: Pharmacies are present in Stone Town and adjacent populous places, providing prescriptions and over-the-counter items.

Medical Evacuation: For urgent medical crises that cannot be managed locally, medical evacuation to mainland Tanzania or other adjacent countries may be necessary. It's crucial to have comprehensive travel insurance that covers medical evacuations.

Health Precautions for Travelers:

Travel Insurance: Before traveling to Zanzibar, buy comprehensive travel insurance that covers medical coverage and emergency medical evacuation.

Prescription drugs: If you are on any prescription drugs, ensure you have a enough supply for the duration of your stay.

Insect Protection: Use insect repellents and mosquito netting to protect against mosquito bites, especially during the evenings and nights.

Emergency Contacts: Carry emergency contact information for local medical institutions and your country's embassy or consulate in Tanzania.

In conclusion, Zanzibar provides a unique and beautiful vacation experience, but it's crucial to be prepared and take required health measures. Staying knowledgeable about the region's health issues, accessing medical services when needed, and taking preventative steps can assist guarantee a safe and pleasurable journey to this wonderful island.

Communication and Internet

Communication and internet connectivity play a crucial role in modern society, providing worldwide connectedness and enabling smooth interactions between individuals, organizations, and governments. In Zanzibar, like many areas of the world, communication and internet infrastructure have expanded swiftly, contributing to socio-economic growth and boosting people's lives.

Mobile Communication: Mobile communication is the principal means of communication in Zanzibar. The island has a well-established mobile network with many operators offering phone calls, text messaging, and mobile broadband services. SIM cards are generally accessible for purchase, and you may select from several prepaid and postpaid plans based on your needs.

Internet Connectivity: Zanzibar's internet connectivity has increased dramatically in recent years. The island has a rising number of internet service providers (ISPs) offering both fixed-line and mobile data services. Internet cafés and Wi-Fi hotspots are accessible in metropolitan centers and famous tourist sites, allowing quick access to the internet for locals and visitors alike.

Internet Speed and Reliability: While big towns and tourism destinations normally have stable internet connectivity, rural locations may have restricted access and poorer internet speeds. However, initiatives to upgrade infrastructure and increase coverage are continuing, seeking to bridge the digital divide and promote internet accessible across the island.

Mobile Data Usage: Many locals and visitors rely on mobile data to remain connected on the go. With the rising availability of 4G and even 5G networks, mobile data consumption for surfing, social networking, and other online activities has become more comfortable and efficient.

Social Media and Messaging Apps: Social media platforms and messaging apps are widely utilized in Zanzibar, just like in other parts of the world. Apps like WhatsApp, Facebook, Instagram, and Twitter are popular for communicating, sharing updates, and staying connected with friends and family.

Internet and E-Commerce: The expanding internet connectivity has also enabled the emergence of e-commerce in Zanzibar. Online marketplaces and local companies sell items and services online, allowing people to buy from the convenience of their homes.

obstacles: Despite tremendous advances, numerous obstacles remain in Zanzibar's communication and internet landscape. Limited internet access in rural regions, periodic network failures, and changes in internet speeds are among the challenges that are being addressed to increase overall connectivity.

Future Developments: Zanzibar, like Tanzania as a whole, is consistently investing in strengthening communication and internet infrastructure. Projects aiming at extending coverage, enhancing data speeds, and encouraging digital literacy are undertaken to build a connected and technologically-enabled society.

In conclusion, communication and internet connectivity have become fundamental to daily life in Zanzibar. The proliferation of mobile networks, internet services, and digital platforms has altered how individuals interact, do business, and obtain information. As technology continues to evolve, Zanzibar is set to harness the promise of the digital era for future socio-economic growth and development.

Safety Precautions

Safety measures are needed to protect yourself and others from potential hazards and risks in various scenarios. Whether at home, on the road, or during outdoor activities, following safety principles may considerably minimize the chance of accidents and create a secure atmosphere for everyone involved. Here are some common safety considerations to keep in mind:

1. Home Safety:

*Install smoke detectors and carbon monoxide detectors in important places of your house.

*Keep fire extinguishers accessible and understand how to use them appropriately.

*Secure your house with trustworthy locks and a home security system.

*Keep dangerous chemicals, sharp objects, and medications out of reach of youngsters.

*Regularly examine and maintain electrical appliances and wiring.

2. Road Safety:

*Always wear seatbelts whether driving or riding in a vehicle.

*Observe speed limits and traffic restrictions.

*Avoid using electronic gadgets while driving.

*Never drink and drive.

*Use crosswalks and pedestrian crossings when walking.

3. Outdoor Safety:

*Wear adequate protection gear when engaged in sports or recreational activities.

*Stay hydrated and use sunscreen when spending time outdoors.

*Be wary of weather conditions and seek cover during storms or excessive heat.

*Follow guidelines and warnings at beaches and swimming areas.

*Inform someone about your outside intentions and approximate return time.

4. Fire Safety:

*Educate yourself and your family on fire escape strategies and meeting spots.

*Keep candles and open flames away from combustible things.

*Never leave cooking alone in the kitchen.

*Keep a fire extinguisher easily available.

5. Travel Safety:

*Research and be informed of the safety conditions in your vacation location.

*Keep your possessions secure and avoid flaunting valuables in public.

*Use trustworthy transportation options and avoid unauthorized taxis.

*Keep copies of key documents in a different area from the originals.

6. Water Safety:

*Ensure sufficient supervision for youngsters around water bodies, including pools and beaches.

*Use life jackets or personal flotation devices when boating or participating in water sports.

*Learn basic water rescue methods.

7. First Aid and Emergency Preparedness:

*Familiarize oneself with basic first aid methods.

*Keep a first aid kit at home and in your car.

*Know emergency contact numbers and addresses.

8. Cybersecurity:

*Use secure and unique passwords for online accounts.

*Be cautious about providing personal information online.

*Keep your devices and software up to date with the newest security updates.

*Remember that safety is a shared responsibility, and everyone should actively engage in encouraging safe habits and watching out for one another.

*Taking modest steps may make a major difference in reducing accidents and fostering a secure atmosphere for everyone.

CHAPTER 10: SOUVENIRS AND MEMENTOS

Shopping in Zanzibar

Shopping in Zanzibar is a fascinating experience that allows tourists to explore the island's bustling marketplaces, unique stores, and native crafts. From spices to handcrafted goods, Zanzibar provides a varied selection of shopping choices that cater to all tastes and interests. Here are some of the shopping hotspots in Zanzibar:

1. Spice shops: Zanzibar is well known as the "Spice Island," and a visit to its spice shops is a must for any tourist. Explore the busy marketplaces loaded with exotic spices including cloves, nutmeg, cinnamon, and vanilla. The brilliant colors and unique smells create a sensory experience that embodies the soul of the island.

2. Handicrafts & Souvenirs: Zanzibar's marketplaces and local stores are bursting with handcrafted souvenirs and distinctive handicrafts. Look look for finely carved wooden sculptures, traditional Maasai beading, handwoven baskets,

and bright textiles. These make great wonderful presents and treasures to take home.

3. Stone Town Market (Darajani Market): Located in the center of Stone Town, the Stone Town Market, also known as Darajani Market, is a busy and chaotic market where you can purchase anything from fresh vegetables to local crafts. It's a fantastic place to buy spices, fresh fruits, vegetables, and fish, as well as textiles and apparel.

4. Forodhani Night Market: As the sun sets, the Forodhani Night Market comes to life along the shoreline in Stone Town. Here, you may experience a variety of traditional street cuisine, including Zanzibari pizzas (chapati with varied toppings), fish skewers, sugar cane juice, and much more. It's a bright setting with a varied choice of cuisines to savor.

5. Malindi Market: Malindi Market is another lively market in Stone Town, offering a wide range of commodities from apparel and textiles to household goods. It's a fantastic spot to purchase for real African textiles and outfits.

6. Mrembo Spa Shop: If you're seeking for locally manufactured beauty goods and spa services, visit the Mrembo Spa Shop in Stone Town. They provide a selection of natural and handcrafted skincare products using Zanzibar's famed spices.

7. Art Galleries: Zanzibar is home to brilliant artists, and you may tour several art galleries in Stone Town, showing local paintings, sculptures, and other artistic expressions. Purchasing artwork helps the local arts community and allows you to carry a bit of Zanzibar's creativity home with you.

8. Beach stores: Along the island's magnificent beaches, you'll discover beachside stores selling a range of apparel, jewelry, and accessories. These boutiques give an opportunity to browse while enjoying the lovely coastline views.

When shopping in Zanzibar, remember to improve your negotiating abilities, as haggling is a popular and accepted part of the shopping culture. It's also crucial to be courteous and considerate while talking with local sellers.

In conclusion, shopping in Zanzibar is a joyful adventure of discovery, where you can immerse yourself in the island's colorful marketplaces and uncover a treasure trove of spices, handcrafted souvenirs, and distinctive local items. Whether you're seeking gifts for loved ones or souvenirs to remember your vacation, shopping in Zanzibar is guaranteed to leave you with cherished memories and physical recollections of this enchanting island.

Unique Gifts to Bring Home

Bringing home unique souvenirs from Zanzibar allows you to share a bit of the island's rich culture and tradition with your loved ones. Here are some unusual and original gift options that express the soul of Zanzibar:

1. Spices & Spice Blends: Zanzibar is known for its fragrant spices. Purchase fresh spices like cloves, nutmeg, cinnamon, and vanilla, or choose for pre-packaged spice mixes that give distinctive tastes to foods. Spices are not only delicious but also a reminder of the island's moniker, the "Spice Island."

2. Handwoven Baskets: Handwoven baskets produced from natural fibers are a popular gift choice. These wonderfully constructed baskets come in various sizes and styles, great for use as storage or decorative items.

3. Traditional Maasai beading: Maasai beading is vivid and eye-catching. Look for beaded jewelry, such as necklaces, bracelets, and earrings, created by Maasai artists. The exquisite bead patterns hold cultural importance and make very great presents.

4. Kanga and Kitenge Fabric: Kanga and kitenge are vibrant and versatile African textiles. They are utilized as apparel, scarves, wraps, and even as wall hangings. Choose from a broad choice of designs and colors to suit your taste.

5. Hand-carved Wooden Sculptures: Zanzibar's experienced craftsmen produce magnificent wooden sculptures, frequently portraying animals, traditional characters, or abstract motifs. These unusual pieces of art make for wonderful home décor items or conversation starters.

6. Zanzibari Spices and Teas: Apart from individual spices, you may get packaged Zanzibari spice mixes and teas. These make for easy and fragrant presents that encapsulate the island's gastronomic flavor.

7. Coconut items: Coconuts are numerous in Zanzibar, and you may get many coconut-based items, such as coconut oil, coconut soap, and coconut shell handicrafts. These objects represent the island's natural riches and are both functional and sustainable.

8. Paintings & Artwork: Explore local art galleries for paintings and artwork by Zanzibari artists. Look for works

that represent the island's beauty, culture, or animals, creating a lasting remembrance of your time in Zanzibar.

9. Tinga Tinga Art: Tinga Tinga art is a lively and colorful type of African art marked by its strong and abstract motifs. Look for Tinga Tinga paintings and prints to bring a touch of African beauty to your house.

10. Traditional Musical Instruments: If you're a music fan or know someone who is, try acquiring traditional Zanzibari musical instruments like the oud or the traditional African drum called ngoma.

When purchasing presents, go for locally manufactured and sustainable products that support local artists and the community. Remember that negotiating is typical in Zanzibar, so don't hesitate to negotiate costs in a civilized manner.

By purchasing unique gifts from Zanzibar, you can share the island's beauty and cultural diversity with your friends and family, while also helping to the preservation of its legacy. These thoughtful and unique presents will definitely be loved and cherished mementos of your time in this wonderful island paradise.

CONCLUSION

In conclusion, Zanzibar is an intriguing and unique location that provides a great combination of history, culture, natural beauty, and adventure. Its rich legacy as a medieval commercial centre is reflected in the beautiful Stone Town, a UNESCO World legacy Site that immerses tourists in its twisting lanes, busy marketplaces, and architectural treasures. The island's cultural tapestry, inspired by African, Arab, Indian, and European traditions, produces a distinctive and colorful environment that enchants people from all corners of the world.

Beyond the cultural appeal, Zanzibar features an abundance of natural beauties that entice explorers and wildlife aficionados. From its sun-kissed beaches with turquoise oceans to its lush tropical woods, Zanzibar shows the finest of island paradise. Snorkeling and diving possibilities abound, with spectacular coral reefs teaming with marine life waiting to be discovered under the seas. Encounter the gorgeous sea turtles, lively dolphins, and the uncommon red colobus monkeys in their native habitats.

The island's dedication to responsible tourism initiatives assures that tourists may enjoy its splendors while contributing to its preservation and the well-being of its residents. Supporting local communities, preserving cultural traditions, and conserving the environment are fundamental values that pave the road for sustainable tourism in Zanzibar.

Zanzibar's culinary pleasures, marrying the best spices and fresh fish, dazzle taste buds with a combination of sensations. Indulge in the fragrant meals and unique dining experiences, reflecting the island's past as the Spice Island.

Zanzibar is not simply a location to visit; it's a destination that embraces tourists with open arms, leaving them with amazing experiences and a profound respect for its beauty and legacy. Whether you want leisure on the sandy shores, discovery of its historical riches, or an immersing experience with its diverse wildlife, Zanzibar has something to offer every wanderlust-filled heart.

As you begin on your journey to this wonderful island, remember to take time to connect with the inhabitants, absorb the cultural subtleties, and embrace the times of peace and adventure. Embrace the island's culture of "pole pole" (slowly) and relish every moment of your Zanzibari adventure.

In essence, Zanzibar is a treasure trove of discovery, giving a sensory voyage through its sights, sounds, tastes, and fragrances. It is an island of dreams, where history whispers its secrets and nature beckons you to go off the usual road. Whether you want romance, adventure, or cultural immersion, Zanzibar awaits with open arms, beckoning you to embark on a trip of a lifetime.

Printed in Great Britain
by Amazon